Through the Eyes of
CHILDREN

NEPAL

Connie Bickman

Published by Abdo & Daughters, 4940 Viking Drive, Suite 622, Edina, Minnesota 55435.

Printed in the United States.

Cover Photo credit: Connie Bickman
Interior Photo credits: Connie Bickman

Edited by Julie Berg

LIBRARY OF CONGRESS CATALOGING-IN-PUBLICATION DATA

Bickman, Connie
    Nepal / Connie Bickman.
       p. cm. -- (Through the eyes of children)
    Includes Index.
    Summary; Looks at how people, especially children, live in Nepal.
work, and other aspects of life in Egypt.

    ISBN 1-56239-549-1 (lib. bdg.)
    1. Nepal -- Juvenile Literature. [1. Nepal -- Social life and customs.]
    I. Berg, Julie. II. Title. III Series.
    DS493.5.B5 1996
    954.96--dc20
                                    95-38546
                                      CIP
                                      AC

Contents

Welcome to Nepal!

Nepal is a beautiful country.
Its capital is the busy city of Kathmandu.
The city is like an ancient museum.
There are beautiful wood-carved temples and buildings.
The outdoor markets look like they did thousands of years ago.

Nepal's snow-covered Himalaya Mountains have eight of the world's ten highest mountains.
The tallest, Mt. Everest, is 29,028 feet (8,848 m) high.
Nepal has valleys of flowered forests and terraced fields.
It also has jungles where tigers, rhinoceroses and elephants live.
It has tall waterfalls, rushing rivers, and calm glass-like lakes that reflect huge mountains.

Nepal is a small country.
The land is sandwiched between India and China.
Some of its neighbors are Tibet, Sikkim, and Bhutan.

The main language is Nepali but many tribes speak their own language.
Some people also speak and understand English.
Nepalese follow their own customs and ways of dressing.
The money they use is called a *rupee*.

More than 18 million people live in Nepal.
The two main ethnic groups are the Indo Aryans and
the Mongolians.
The people are divided into at least 35 ethnic cultures.
Some are the Gurung, Sherpa, Newar, Rai, Brahman,
and Chhetri.
These tribes are also divided into castes.
The caste system determines what a person's
occupation in life will be.

Nepal is a Hindu kingdom.
Nepal is also the birthplace of Buddha.
The two religions, Buddhism and Hinduism, blend
many of the same beliefs.
Tibetan Buddhism is very strong in Nepal.
Many of the people came from Tibet when it was
overtaken by China.
Pictures of their religious leader, the Dalai Lama, are
everywhere.
Religion is a very important part of the people's lives.
It dictates the traditions and daily rituals of the
Nepalese.
Hindu temples and Buddhist shrines are scattered in
the cities, villages, and the countryside.
Praying and making daily offerings of rice and flowers
is common.

Nepal has many ways that are unfamiliar to us.
But many things are also the same.
Let's learn more about the children of Nepal.

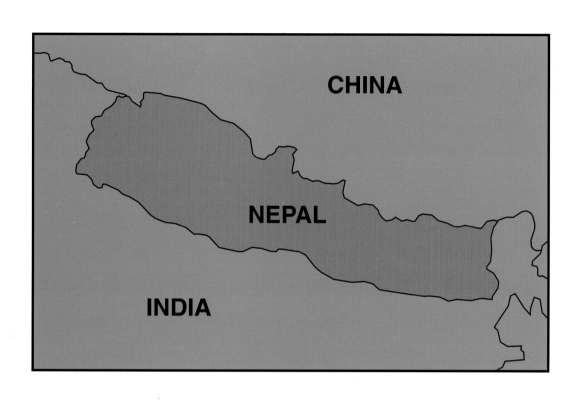

CHINA

NEPAL

INDIA

DETAIL AREA

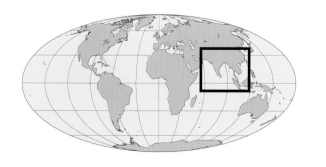 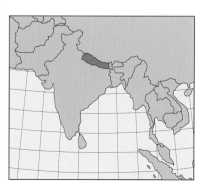

Meet the Children

The children of Nepal spend their day working, playing or as shepherds.

Shepherds take care of the goats and sheep.
Every day they take the animals to a pasture to eat.
The children like to play while the goats and sheep graze.

This girl loves to play at old temples.
She can climb in a friendly jungle of stone animals.
There are many old statues on which to climb.

What's Good to Eat?

The people of Nepal eat a lot of rice.
It is grown everywhere except in high mountain areas.
Vegetables like cauliflower and green beans are also
eaten at meals.

These children are keeping their stove burning.
They burn wood to cook rice.
All of their cooking is done outside on the stove.
It is made of cement and stones.

The Nepali national dish is called *daal bhaat.*
It is boiled rice with lentil sauce and curried vegetables.
In the high mountains, it may be too cold to grow rice.
Instead the farmers grow millet.
It is a type of grain they grind into flour.
With the millet they make *dhiro.*
It is boiled in water to make a thick soup.

This plate is filled with dhiro, and sauce for dipping.
The meal also includes mustard leaves, beans,
cauliflower, cabbage and hot green chili pickles.
In Nepal, many people eat with their fingers instead of
silverware.

Most people in Nepal do not eat beef.
For those who follow the Hindu religion, eating beef is
forbidden.
Buffalo, mutton, chicken, pork, wild boar, and doves
may be eaten.
Meat is expensive and usually prepared only on special
occasions.

What Do They Wear?

Many Nepalese women and young girls wear long flowered cotton skirts called *lungi*.
The white cotton material wrapped around the waist is called a *patuka*.
It keeps the back warm and is a good place to carry snacks and little brothers and sisters.
Many women wear scarves and shawls over their shoulders and heads.

Traditional costumes in Nepal are very colorful.
These dancers wear the dresses from their own clans.
You can tell where a person lives by the clothing they wear.

In Nepal you will see people draped in dark red cloth.
They are Buddhist monks and nuns.
All young boys that are Buddhist must enter a monastery.
Some will become Buddhist monks.
Others will find jobs and have families.

This group of monks and nuns are at Boudhanath Stupa.
It is one of the biggest *stupas*, or temples, in the world.
It is as big as a football field!
It is one of the most famous places in Nepal.
The flags flying in the air are called prayer flags.

Where Do They Live?

Many families in Nepal live in small villages.
Their houses are made of cement and mud.
Often families work where they live.

This family owns a carpet factory.
They make beautiful carpets to sell all over the world.
The carpet industry is Nepal's largest source of income.
Carpets are drying on the roof.

A nun in Nepal is called an *Ani.*
This girl is a ten-year-old Ani.
She was an orphan before the other Anis brought her to live with them.
She has a plate of beautiful flowers to put on the table.

This boy is studying to be a monk in the Hindu religion.
He lives in a very old temple with other monks.

Getting Around

In Nepal people travel by cars and buses.
Others ride bicycles in the city.
One type of taxi is a three-wheel bike.
They are usually brightly painted, and a ride does not cost much.
The taxi must drive around the cow.
Cows are sacred in Nepal and are treated special.
They go wherever they want to!

There are no roads in the mountains.
When traveling in the mountains you must walk.
That is called trekking.
Many people will walk for days to get from village to village.

School is Fun

Many children in Nepal have a long climb to get to school every day.
Their school house is on a mountaintop!
Most classes are outside in the fresh air.
In the villages, boys and girls go to school together.
In the city, boys and girls go to different schools.
Some children don't go to school because they have to help their family farm.

Nepali students learn to speak English.
They also study their own Nepali language.
It is based on an ancient Indian language called
Sanskrit.
They will also learn math, social studies, history and
geography.

School studies are much different for students in a
monastery.
They have their lessons inside a temple.
Their teacher is a lama or a holy man.
Much of their study is called practice.
They practice to understand themselves.
Their teachers say that is the most important lesson to
learn.

How Do They Work?

Children often carry a heavy basket called a *dokko*. They carry food, supplies, and sometimes other children! This girl is hauling millet from the fields. It will be ground into flour.

Boys and girls spread grains out on mats to dry. These children spend most of their time outside.

Children help in the fields at a very young age.
They will have at least three harvests a year.
Potatoes, wheat, corn, sugarcane, fruit, millet, and rice
are the main crops.

Most people in Nepal don't have refrigerators.
They go to the market every day to buy fresh fruit and
vegetables.

Their Land

These mountains are in the Anapurna Range.
They are called the Himalayas.
The name *Himalaya* means "Home of the Gods."
When trekking in the Himalayas, you will see beautiful flowers.
You will see snow covered mountains, and green fields.
You will even trek through areas they call jungle.
There are many villages in the mountains.
Nepal's sacred mountain is called *Machhapuchhare*.
It is also called fishtail, because people think it looks like the tail of a fish.
Because it is sacred, no one can climb this mountain.

The lowland area is called the *Terai* region.
There are swamps and jungle in this part of Nepal.
One famous area is Royal Chitwan National Park.
Here you will see deer, rhinoceroses, Bengal tigers, leopards, crocodiles and even bears!
You will also see people riding elephants.
It is much different than Nepal's mountain and city regions.

Life in the City

These children like to run and ride bikes.
They are in Durbar Square in the ancient city of Bhahtapur.
The city's old temples have beautiful carvings and decorations.
The carved figures usually tell about history.

This modern Tamang mother and daughter are visiting Dubar Square in Kathmandu.

They are sitting by a holy man. He is called a *yogi* or a *saddus*.

The children call him Baba.

The bright designs on his forehead tell what sect or religion he follows.

A famous temple of Nepal is Swayambhunath Stupa.
It is over 2,000 years old.
To get there you must climb 365 steps.
The eyes of Buddha are on all four sides of this stupa.
They symbolize the all-seeing eyes of Buddha.
This stupa is also called the Monkey Temple because monkeys live around it.

Family Living

Older sisters and brothers often care for babies.
Taking care of her little brother is this girl's job.
She must do it every day while her parents are in the field.
Carrying babies in cloth on the back is very common.

These children also help their mother.
They live in a small village.
Family life is very important in Nepal.

Children are the Same

It is fun to see how children in other countries live. They may work, travel and dress different than you. Children may play and go to school and have families just like you.

One thing is always the same. That is a smile. If you smile at other children, they will smile back.
That is how you make new friends.
It is fun to have new friends all over the world!

"Dhanyabad." Thank you for visiting with the children of Nepal.
"Namaste."

Glossary

Anapurna (An-a-PURN-a) - mountain range in the Himalayas.

Ani (AWN-e) - a Buddhist nun

Baba (BAA-baa) - holy man

Bhaai Tika (Bai TI-ka) - worship ceremony of the brother. Sisters perform puja for their brother's long lives. The last day of the Festival of Lights.

Bhaktapur (BACK-ta-pur) - one of the main cities in Kathmandu Valley.

Boudhanath (BOW-dan-ath) - one of the largest stupas in the world.

Buddha (BOO-da) - Buddha was a man named Siddhartha Gautama who studied to become perfect. A spiritually enlightened person.

Buddhism (BOO-dism) - a religion based on the teachings of Buddha.

Caste (Cast) - Hindu religious and social system dividing people into four main castes. Brahman - priests, Kshatriya or Chhetri - noble warriors, Vaisya - merchants or farmers, and Sudra - worker.

Daal Bhaat (DAL Baat) - the Napali national dish of boiled rice, lentil sauce and curried vegetables.

Dalai Lama (DAL-a LA-ma) - Incarnate (reborn) leader of Tibetan Buddhism.

Dhanyabad (DA-nay-baat) - "Thank you" in Nepali.

Dharamsala (DAR-am-sal-a) - City in India where the Dalai Lama lives.

Dhiro (DI-ro) - a type of mush made from millet or corn.

Dokko (DO-ko) - large wicker baskets used for carrying supplies.

Durbar Square (DUR-bar) - plazas filled with temples in Kathmandu Valley's three main cities, Kathmandu, Petan, and Bhaktapur.

Festival of Lights - a five day celebration. The first two days honor the messengers, the crow and the dog. The third day honors the sacred cow, the fourth day is the bull and the fifth day the brother.

Gurkha (GUR-ka) - Nepali soldiers in the Indian and British armies, famous for being good fighters.

Gurung (GUR-ung), **Sherpa** (SHER-pa), **Newar** (KNEE-waar), **Rai, Brahman** (BRA-man), **Chhetri** (CHET-ri), **Tamang** (Tam-ONG), - Some of the ethnic groups or tribes of people who live in Nepal.

Himalaya (Him-al-A-ya) - a mountain range that runs through Nepal.

Hindu (HIN-du) - a native of India who practices Hinduism.

Hinduism - a religion based on the nature of the individual self.

Indo Aryan (IN-do AR-an) - people who come from India.

Kathmandu (Kat-man-DU) - the capital of Nepal.

Khukuri (Kur-KUR-e) - curved knife used by Gurkha soldiers.

Lama (LA-ma) - a Tibetan Buddhist spiritual leader.

Lungi (LUN-gi) - long usually flowered cotton fabric wrapped around as a skirt.

Machhapuchhare (Ma-cha-PUCH-rae) - Fishtail. The sacred mountain in the Himalayas.

Mantra (MAN-tra) - words chanted as a prayer.

Millet (MIL-et) - type of grain.

Monastery (MONA-ster-y) - a temple for spiritual study.

Mongolian (Mon-GO-li-an) people who come from Chinese and Tibetan ancestors.

Mt. Everest - the highest mountain in the world.

Namaste (NA-ma-stae) - Napali for "hello," "welcome" and "goodbye."

Patuka (Pa-TU-ka) - cotton material wrapped around the waist to help carry loads.

Royal Chitwan National Park (CHIT-wan) - a wildlife reserve in the Terai region with grasslands, forests and lakes.

Rupee (RU-pee) - Napali money.

Saddhu (SAD-u) - Hindu holy man who wanders, begs, and prays.

Sanskrit (SAN-skrit) - ancient Indian language that the Napali language is based on.

Sherpa (ShER-pa) - the word is sometimes used to describe a trekking helper or porter.

Stupa (STU-pa) - a domed Buddhist temple.

Swayambhunath Stupa (SWAM-bu-nath) - sometimes called the Monkey Temple.

Terai (Ter-AI) - lowland regions.

Tika (TIK-a) - red vermillion powder that is put on the forehead.

Topi (TO-pi) - traditional hat worn by Nepalese males - named for the fabric it is made from.

Trekking (TREK-ing) - walking in the mountains.

Yogi (YO-gi) - holy man or teacher.

Index

About the Author/Photographer

Connie Bickman is a photojournalist whose photography has won regional and international awards.

She is retired from a ten-year newspaper career and currently owns her own portrait studio and art gallery. She also is an active freelance photographer and writer who travels the far corners of the world to photograph native cultures.

Connie is a member of the National Press Association and the Minnesota Newspaper Photographers Association.